In Sweden
En Suecia

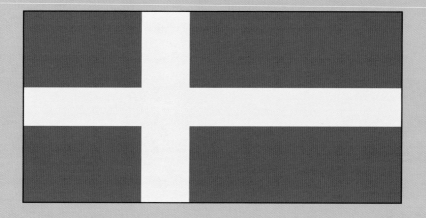

written by **Judy Zocchi** illustrated by **Neale Brodie**

dingles&company New Jersey

For Rocky & Robbin

First printing

PUBLISHED BY dingles&company
P.O. Box 508 • Sea Girt, New Jersey • 08750
WEBSITE: www.dingles.com • E-MAIL: info@dingles.com

Library of Congress Catalog Card No.: 2004096611
ISBN: 1-59646-088-1

Printed in the United States of America

ART DIRECTION & DESIGN BY Barbie Lambert
ENGLISH EDITED BY Andrea Curley
SPANISH EDITED BY Teresa Carbajal Ravet
RESEARCH AND ADDITIONAL COPY WRITTEN BY Robert Neal Kanner
EDUCATIONAL CONSULTANT Bridget Riley Turnbach
PRE-PRESS BY Pixel Graphics

The Global Adventures series takes children on an around-the-world exploration of a variety of fascinating countries. The series examines each country's history and physical features as well as its most popular customs, activities, and foods.

Global Adventures

Judy Zocchi

is the author of the Global Adventures, Holiday Happenings, Click & Squeak's Computer Basics, and Paulie and Sasha series. She is a writer and lyricist who holds a bachelor's degree in fine arts/theater from Mount Saint Mary's College and a master's degree in educational theater from New York University. She lives in Manasquan, New Jersey, with her husband, David.

Neale Brodie

is a freelance illustrator who lives in Brighton, England, with his wife and young daughter. He is a self-taught artist, having received no formal education in illustration. As well as illustrating a number of children's books, he has worked as an animator in the computer games industry.

In Sweden people spend the KRONA.

Krona is the official currency of Sweden. One krona equals 100 ore. In English krona means crown.

La KRONA es lo que la gente de Suecia usa como moneda.

La krona es la moneda oficial de Suecia. Una krona vale 100 oere. En inglés krona significa corona.

CRYSTAL is made and sold worldwide.

Sweden was one of the first countries to make crystal and glass. The southeastern region of Sweden has approximately twenty world famous glassworks and is called the Kingdom of Crystal.

Se hace CRISTAL y se vende por todo el mundo.

Suecia fue uno de los primeros países que hacía cristal y vidrio. La región del sureste de Suecia tiene aproximadamente veinte vidrierías famosas por todo el mundo y se conoce como el Reino del Cristal.

SWEDISH
is what people speak.

Swedish is the official language of Sweden.

SUECO
es lo que la gente habla.

El sueco es el idioma oficial de Suecia.

What happened? ¿Qué pasó?
I went too fast on the turn. Venía muy rápido por la vuelta.

An **ICE HOTEL** guest sleeps on a reindeer's hide.

Every year since 1989 a hotel is built entirely of ice in Jukkasjarvi, a village in northern Sweden. It has an ice wedding chapel, an ice art exhibition hall, a movie theater with an ice screen, and rooms for more than 100 guests. The hotel only lasts for 6 months, though, because in summer it melts!

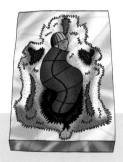

Un huésped del **HOTEL DE HIELO** duerme sobre la piel de reno.

Desde 1989, cada año un hotel se construye enteramente de hielo en Jukkasjarvi, una aldea en Suecia del norte. Tiene una capilla de hielo para bodas, un salón de hielo para exponer arte, una sala de cine con pantalla de hielo y habitaciones para más de 100 huéspedes. ¡Sin embargo, el hotel sólo dura 6 meses porque en el verano se derrite!

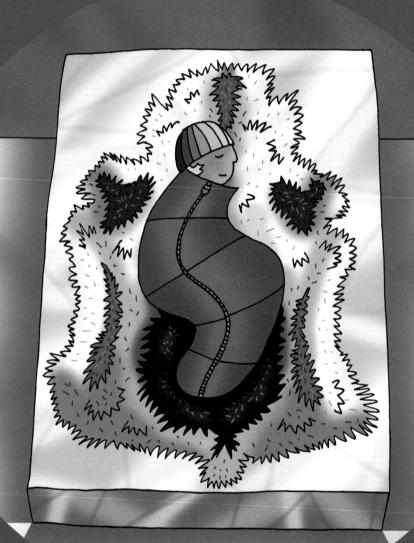

In Sweden
SAINT LUCIA'S DAY
is a favorite holiday.

Saint Lucia's Day is celebrated on December 13. Because Saint Lucia died at the time of year when nights begin to get shorter, she became a symbol of light to the Swedish people. The holiday also celebrates the coming of Christmas.

En Suecia
el DÍA DE SANTA LUCIA
es el día festivo favorito.

El Día de Santa Lucia se celebra el 13 de diciembre. Santa Lucia murió durante la temporada del año en la cual las noches empiezan a ser más cortas, ella llegó a simbolizar la luz para la gente sueca. El día festivo también celebra la llegada de la Navidad.

A SUMMERLAND is a popular outdoor gathering place.

This recreational area offers the entire family many activities, including swimming, row boating, bicycling, and water rides in beautifully landscaped surroundings.

Un SUMMERLAND es un lugar popular al aire libre para las reuniones.

Esta área recreativa ofrece muchas actividades para la familia entera, inclusive la natación, el paseo en bote, el paseo en bicicleta y los paseos en agua en las afueras bellamente ajardinadas.

The WOLVERINE is a cross between a weasel and a bear.

A member of the weasel family, wolverines walk on the soles of their feet just as bears do. When there is snow on the ground, their large, furry feet act like snowshoes, allowing the animal to move quickly to capture its prey.

El animal WOLVERINE es una mezcla entre una comadreja y un oso.

Como un miembro de la familia de las comadrejas, los wolverines caminan en las suelas de los pies así como los osos. Cuando hay nieve en la tierra, sus patas grandes y peludas sirven como raquetas para la nieve y permiten el movimiento rápido para capturar la presa.

A SMORGASBORD
takes up lots of space.

This is a Swedish style of serving meals to large numbers of people, such as at a party. It usually consists of a long table set with a variety of dishes, such as herring (a type of small fish), meatballs, salmon, breads, salads, potatoes, and desserts.

Un SMORGASBORD
ocupa mucho espacio.

Este es un estilo sueco de servir comida para un gran número de gente, como para una fiesta. Usualmente consiste de una mesa larga con una variedad de platos, como el arenque (un tipo de pescado fresco), albóndigas, salmón, panes, ensaladas, papas y postres.

In Sweden DALA HORSES are brightly painted.

These carved wooden toy horses were first created by Swedish woodcutters in a region called Dalarna many centuries ago. The horses vary in size, with no two ever identical. They have become a traditional hand-crafted Swedish keepsake.

En Suecia los CABALLOS DALA se pintan brillantemente.

Estos caballos tallados de madera para juguetes fueron creados primeramente por los taladores suecos en la región llamada Dalarna muchos siglos antes. Los caballos varían en tamaño sin que dos sean idénticos. Han llegado a ser un recuerdo sueco tradicional hecho a mano.

VASA is an ancient ship.

In 1628 the Swedish king launched a large warship that was badly designed and sunk a short distance from shore. In 1961 the ship was brought up from the bottom of the ocean almost intact. It is on display in a museum in a Stockholm harbor.

El VASA
es un barco antiguo.

En 1628 el rey sueco lanzó un navío grande de guerra que estaba diseñado muy mal y se hundió a poca distancia de la costa. En 1961 se recupero el navío del fondo del océano casi intacto. Está exhibido en un museo del puerto de Estocolmo.

Students wear WHITE HATS when they graduate.

In Sweden, a white cap is a traditional symbol of learning. Students who finish the Swedish equivalent of high school sometimes wear this traditional graduation cap during the graduation ceremony.

Los estudiantes llevan GORRAS BLANCAS cuando se gradúan.

En Suecia, una gorra blanca es un símbolo tradicional del aprendizaje. Los estudiantes quienes cumplen lo equivalente de la secundaria en Suecia algunas veces llevan esta gorra tradicional de graduación durante la ceremonia de graduación.

BLUEBERRY SOUP
is given to skiers to sip.

This popular soup is made with fresh blueberries, water, sugar, and lemon. It is usually kept warm in a thermos and served on the slopes for refreshment.

El CALDO DE ARÁNDANOS
se les sirve a los esquiadores para sorber.

Este caldo popular se hace con arándanos frescos, agua, azúcar y limón. Usualmente se mantiene caliente en termos y se sirve en las pistas de esquí como bebida.

Swedish culture is fun to learn.

La cultura sueca es divertida para aprender.

KRONA
(KRO-na)

CRYSTAL

SWEDISH

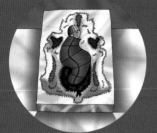

ICE HOTEL

SAINT LUCIA'S DAY

SUMMERLAND

WOLVERINE

SMORGASBORD
(smor-gose-BORD)

DALA HORSES
(DAW-la)

VASA

WHITE HATS

BLUEBERRY SOUP

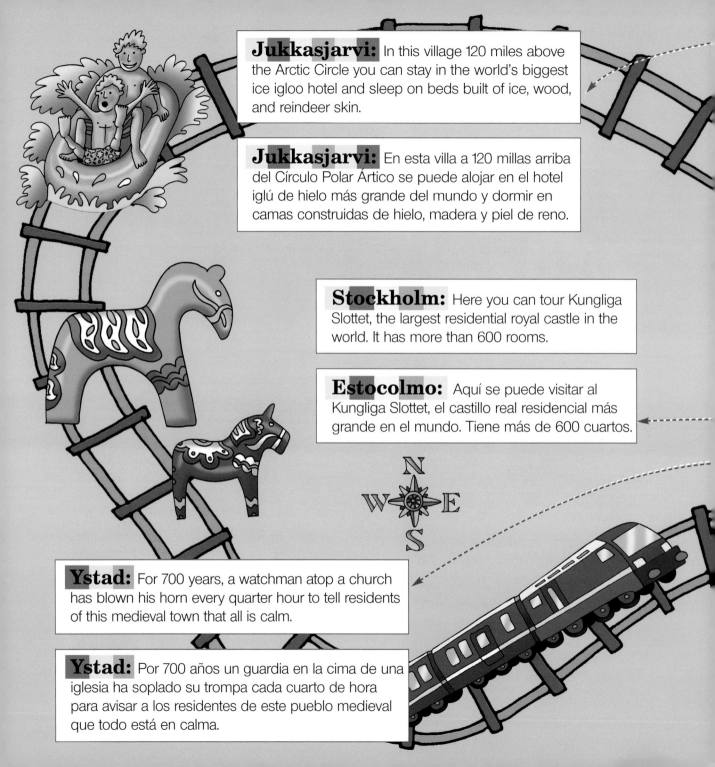

Jukkasjarvi: In this village 120 miles above the Arctic Circle you can stay in the world's biggest ice igloo hotel and sleep on beds built of ice, wood, and reindeer skin.

Jukkasjarvi: En esta villa a 120 millas arriba del Círculo Polar Ártico se puede alojar en el hotel iglú de hielo más grande del mundo y dormir en camas construidas de hielo, madera y piel de reno.

Stockholm: Here you can tour Kungliga Slottet, the largest residential royal castle in the world. It has more than 600 rooms.

Estocolmo: Aquí se puede visitar al Kungliga Slottet, el castillo real residencial más grande en el mundo. Tiene más de 600 cuartos.

Ystad: For 700 years, a watchman atop a church has blown his horn every quarter hour to tell residents of this medieval town that all is calm.

Ystad: Por 700 años un guardia en la cima de una iglesia ha soplado su trompa cada cuarto de hora para avisar a los residentes de este pueblo medieval que todo está en calma.

NORWAY

SWEDEN

Jukkasjarvi

GULF OF BOTHNIA

FINLAND

Stockholm

NORTH SEA

Ystad

BALTIC SEA

See what you can discover at every turn!

¡Mira qué puedes descubrir por cada vuelta!

OFFICIAL NAME:
Kingdom of Sweden

CAPITAL CITY:
Stockholm

CURRENCY:
Swedish krona

MAJOR LANGUAGE:
Swedish

BORDERS:
Finland, Gulf of Bothnia, Baltic Sea, Norway

CONTINENT:
Europe

ABOUT SWEDEN

The first inhabitants were hunter tribes who came from what is now Europe by way of a land bridge. In the 11th century, Norse people, or Vikings, who lived in the area controlled the river trade. They also went on expeditions to trade with or conquer other lands. In the 14th century, Sweden united with Norway and Denmark under one king but broke away in the 16th century. In 1809 Sweden became a constitutional monarchy (where the king's or queen's powers are limited by a set of rules, or constitution). Sweden remained neutral in both World War I and II. The country has about 90,000 lakes and is three-fifths forests. Fifteen percent of Sweden is north of the Arctic Circle. Major industries include lumbering, mining, and tourism. Sweden is known for its social welfare system, where the government provides social services for all of its citizens.

UNDERSTANDING AND CELEBRATING CULTURAL DIFFERENCES
• What do you have in common with children from Sweden?
• What things do you do differently from the children in Sweden?
• What is your favorite new thing you learned about Sweden?
• What unique thing about your culture would you like to share?

TRAVELING THROUGH SWEDEN
• Can you name the country that borders Sweden to the east?
• In which direction would you be traveling if you journeyed from Stockholm to Jonkoping?
• In which region of Sweden is the Arctic Circle located?

TRY SOMETHING NEW...
Have a Viking party and make your own hats. You can make a Viking hat from construction paper or a paper oatmeal canister. Don't forget to add horns! Then dress up in the type of clothing that Vikings might have worn.